REWIRE YOUR MIND

Enhance Mood, Boost Memory

CHANGE YOUR HABITS

Energize Your Life and Sharpen Focus

TRANSFORM YOUR BRAIN

While Strengthening Relationship

By: Brooke Richardson and Lartina Jones

L.B. George Books

This book provides practical insights, exercises, and strategies to help readers achieve mental clarity, emotional balance, and improved relationships through the power of mind rewiring. Not to be used for medical diagnosis.

Table of Contents:

Introduction

Understanding the Power of Mind Rewiring

In the fast-paced world we navigate today, our minds are constantly bombarded with information, demands, and distractions. It's easy to feel overwhelmed, unfocused, and emotionally drained. Yet, within each of us lies a remarkable capability: the ability to rewire our minds.

Mind rewiring is not a mysterious or esoteric concept but rather a scientifically grounded approach to enhancing our mental and emotional well-being. It involves leveraging the brain's neuroplasticity—the ability of the brain to reorganize itself by forming new neural connections throughout life. This phenomenon allows us to learn, adapt, and change habits well into adulthood.

At the core of mind rewiring is the understanding that our thoughts, emotions, and behaviors are interconnected. By deliberately changing our thought patterns and behaviors, we can create profound shifts in our mood, memory, habits, and overall life satisfaction.

This book, "Rewire Your Mind," is a comprehensive guide crafted to empower you with practical tools and insights to embark on this transformative journey. Whether you seek to enhance your mood, boost your memory, change detrimental habits, or strengthen your relationships, this book offers a roadmap. Through scientifically backed strategies, mindfulness practices, and cognitive behavioral techniques, you will learn how to harness the power of your brain to achieve lasting positive change.

Throughout these pages, you will find exercises, anecdotes, and real-life examples that illustrate the principles of mind rewiring in action. Each chapter builds upon the last, guiding you through the process step-by-step, from understanding the basics to implementing advanced techniques.

By embracing the principles of neuroplasticity and mind rewiring, you are not only investing in your own well-being but also unlocking your potential for growth and fulfillment. Whether you're seeking clarity in your thoughts, resilience in the face of challenges, or deeper connections with others, the journey starts here.

Join us on this transformative path as we explore how to enhance mood, boost memory, change habits, energize life, sharpen focus, and strengthen relationships through the power of mind rewiring. Together, let's embark on a journey of self-discovery and empowerment.

Chapter 1:

Enhancing Mood Through Positive Thinking

The way we think profoundly influences how we feel and behave. In this chapter, we delve into the powerful impact of positive thinking on enhancing mood and overall well-being.

Positive thinking isn't just about ignoring challenges or putting on a smile in tough times. It's a mindset that allows us to approach life with optimism, resilience, and a proactive attitude. Research in psychology has shown that cultivating positive thoughts can reduce stress levels, lower the risk of depression, and even improve physical health.

We'll explore practical strategies for adopting a positive mindset, including mindfulness techniques, gratitude practices, and reframing negative thoughts. By learning to challenge pessimistic beliefs and cultivate a more optimistic outlook, you can transform how you experience daily life.

Throughout this chapter, we'll provide exercises and examples to help you apply these techniques in your own life. Whether you're facing setbacks at work, navigating personal relationships, or simply seeking more joy and fulfillment, the principles discussed here will empower you to take charge of your mood and emotional well-being.

By the end of Chapter 1, you'll have a deeper understanding of how positive thinking can enhance your mood and set the stage for further transformations in your journey to rewire your mind.

Adopting a Positive Mindset

Adopting a positive mindset is more than just a fleeting feeling of happiness; it's a fundamental shift in how we perceive and interact with the world around us. This chapter explores practical strategies rooted in mindfulness, gratitude, and cognitive reframing to help you cultivate optimism and resilience in your daily life.

Understanding Mindfulness Techniques

Mindfulness involves paying attention to the present moment without judgment. By practicing mindfulness, you can become more aware of your thoughts and emotions, allowing you to respond thoughtfully rather than react impulsively. Techniques such as mindful breathing, body scan meditations, and mindful eating can help anchor you in the present and reduce stress and anxiety.

Practical Strategies for Mindfulness

Begin incorporating mindfulness into your daily routine with simple practices like taking mindful walks, setting aside dedicated time for meditation, or using apps that guide you through mindfulness exercises. These practices enhance self-awareness and build resilience, enabling you to navigate challenges with greater clarity and calm.

Embracing Gratitude Practices

Gratitude involves consciously appreciating the positive aspects of your life, no matter how small. Regularly practicing gratitude can shift your focus from what's lacking to what you have, fostering a sense of abundance and well-being. Keeping a gratitude journal, expressing thanks to others, or reflecting on three good things each day are effective ways to cultivate gratitude.

Implementing Gratitude in Daily Life

Integrate gratitude into your routine by starting or ending each day with a gratitude practice. Notice the positive moments throughout your day, however mundane they may seem, and take a moment to acknowledge and appreciate them. Over time, this habit rewires your brain to default to a positive outlook, even in challenging circumstances.

Reframing Negative Thoughts

Negative thoughts and beliefs can cloud our perception and dampen our mood. Reframing involves consciously challenging and replacing negative thoughts with more realistic and positive ones. Techniques like cognitive restructuring, thought challenging worksheets, and perspective-taking exercises help you identify and modify unhelpful thought patterns.

Strategies for Cognitive Reframing

Practice cognitive reframing by recognizing negative thought patterns as they arise. Ask yourself whether these thoughts are realistic and how you might view the situation differently. Replace negative self-talk with affirmations or alternative perspectives that are grounded in evidence and optimism.

Cultivating Optimism and Resilience

Optimism is the belief that good things will happen in the future, while resilience is the ability to bounce back from adversity. By cultivating optimism through positive self-talk, setting realistic goals, and viewing setbacks as opportunities for growth, you strengthen your resilience and ability to navigate life's challenges with grace and determination.

Integrating Strategies into Daily Life

Integrate these strategies into your daily life by creating a personalized routine that incorporates mindfulness, gratitude, and cognitive reframing exercises. Consistency is key to reaping the benefits of these practices, so commit to regular practice and monitor your progress over time.

Embracing a Positive Mindset

Adopting a positive mindset is a journey that requires patience, self-compassion, and dedication. By incorporating mindfulness techniques, gratitude practices, and reframing negative thoughts into your daily routine, you can transform how you experience daily life. Embrace the power of positivity to cultivate resilience, enhance well-being, and foster meaningful connections with yourself and others.

Enhancing mood through positive thinking involves adopting a mindset that focuses on optimism, gratitude, and resilience. Here are some practical examples and strategies:

1. **Gratitude Journaling**: Regularly writing down things you are grateful for can shift your focus towards positive aspects of your life, enhancing feelings of contentment and happiness.

2. **Positive Affirmations**: Using affirmations that reinforce positive beliefs about yourself and your abilities can boost self-esteem and cultivate a more optimistic outlook.

3. **Mindful Awareness**: Practicing mindfulness helps you observe your thoughts and emotions without judgment, promoting a sense of calm and reducing negative thinking patterns.

4. **Focusing on Solutions**: Instead of dwelling on problems, focus on identifying solutions and taking proactive steps towards resolving challenges, which can empower and uplift your mood.

5. **Surrounding Yourself with Positivity**: Spending time with supportive and positive people can influence your mood positively, fostering a sense of connection and well-being.

6. **Physical Activity**: Engaging in regular exercise releases endorphins, which are natural mood elevators, contributing to a more positive mindset.

7. **Limiting Negative Inputs**: Being mindful of the media and information you consume can help reduce exposure to negative news and opinions that may impact your mood adversely.

8. **Visualization**: Visualizing positive outcomes and success in various aspects of your life can instill confidence, motivation, and a sense of accomplishment.

9. **Acts of Kindness**: Performing acts of kindness towards others can generate feelings of fulfillment and happiness, enhancing your overall mood.

10. **Setting Realistic Goals**: Setting achievable goals and celebrating small successes along the way can create a sense of progress and boost optimism about the future.

By incorporating these practices into your daily routine, you can cultivate a more positive mindset and enhance your mood, ultimately leading to greater overall well-being and resilience in the face of challenges.

Chapter 2:

Techniques to Boost Memory and Cognitive Function

Memory and cognitive function are vital aspects of our daily lives, influencing everything from learning new skills to making informed decisions. This chapter explores effective techniques and strategies to enhance memory retention, improve cognitive abilities, and optimize mental performance.

Understanding Memory and Cognitive Function

Memory encompasses the processes involved in encoding, storing, and retrieving information. Cognitive function refers to mental processes such as attention, reasoning, problem-solving, and decision-making. Both memory and cognitive function can be enhanced through targeted practices and lifestyle adjustments.

Importance of Memory and Cognitive Health

Maintaining optimal memory and cognitive function is crucial for productivity, academic success, and overall quality of life. As we age, these abilities may naturally decline, making proactive measures to boost memory and cognitive function essential for long-term mental well-being.

Lifestyle Factors Affecting Memory

Healthy lifestyle habits, including regular physical exercise, adequate sleep, a balanced diet rich in antioxidants and omega-3 fatty acids, and stress management, play significant roles in supporting brain health and enhancing memory retention.

Cognitive Exercises and Brain Training

Engaging in cognitive exercises and brain training activities, such as puzzles, crosswords, Sudoku, and memory games, stimulates neural pathways and enhances cognitive flexibility, attention span, and problem-solving skills.

Strategies to Boost Memory Retention

Utilize mnemonic devices, visualization techniques, and chunking strategies to improve memory retention and recall. These methods help organize information into meaningful patterns or associations, making it easier to retain and retrieve information when needed.

Enhancing Cognitive Abilities through Learning

Continuously challenging your brain with new information and skills, such as learning a musical instrument, a new language, or engaging in lifelong learning opportunities, promotes neuroplasticity and strengthens cognitive abilities over time.

Mindfulness and Cognitive Function

Incorporate mindfulness practices, such as meditation and mindful breathing exercises, to enhance attentional control, reduce cognitive decline, and improve overall cognitive function by promoting focus and mental clarity.

Nutrition and Supplements for Cognitive Health

Explore dietary strategies that support brain health, including foods rich in antioxidants, vitamins, and minerals. Consider supplements like omega-3 fatty acids, vitamin B complex, and ginkgo biloba, known for their cognitive-enhancing properties.

Sleep and Memory Consolidation

Prioritize quality sleep to facilitate memory consolidation and optimize cognitive processing. Adequate sleep supports the brain's ability to encode and store information effectively, enhancing learning and memory retention.

Embracing Techniques for Optimal Cognitive Function

By implementing these techniques and strategies to boost memory and enhance cognitive function into your daily routine, you can optimize mental performance, support long-term brain health, and enjoy greater cognitive vitality throughout life. Embrace the journey of continuous learning and cognitive enrichment to cultivate a sharper mind and enrich your overall quality of life.

Boosting memory and cognitive function involves adopting various techniques and practices that stimulate the brain and enhance its ability to process and retain information. Here are some effective examples:

1. **Memory Palaces (Method of Loci)**: Visualize a familiar place and associate each item you want to remember with specific locations within that place. This technique leverages spatial memory to enhance recall.
2. **Mnemonic Devices**: Use acronyms, rhymes, or chunking (grouping information into smaller, manageable units) to

aid memory retention. Mnemonics make information more memorable by creating associations or patterns.

3. **Repetition and Spacing**: Practice active recall by reviewing information at spaced intervals rather than cramming. Spacing out study or practice sessions helps strengthen memory retention over time.

4. **Visualization**: Create mental images or diagrams to represent information you want to remember. Visualizing concepts or sequences can enhance encoding and recall by engaging visual memory pathways.

5. **Mind Mapping**: Create visual diagrams or maps that represent relationships between ideas or concepts. Mind maps help organize information hierarchically and facilitate understanding and memory retrieval.

6. **Association Techniques**: Link new information with existing knowledge or personal experiences to create meaningful associations. This technique enhances memory consolidation by connecting new information with familiar concepts.

7. **Dual N-Back Training**: Engage in cognitive training exercises, like dual n-back tasks, that challenge working memory. These exercises improve the brain's ability to hold and manipulate information in real-time.

8. **Physical Exercise**: Regular aerobic exercise improves blood flow to the brain, promoting neurogenesis (formation of new neurons) and enhancing cognitive function, including memory and attention.

9. **Sleep Optimization**: Prioritize adequate sleep to support memory consolidation and cognitive processing. Quality sleep enhances learning retention and problem-solving abilities by allowing the brain to organize and store information effectively.

10. **Nutritional Support**: Consume a balanced diet rich in antioxidants, omega-3 fatty acids, and vitamins essential for brain health. Foods like fish, nuts, fruits, and vegetables provide nutrients that support cognitive function and memory.

By incorporating these techniques into your daily routine, you can effectively boost memory and cognitive function, leading to improved learning abilities, sharper focus, and enhanced overall brain health. Adjust these techniques based on personal preferences and specific learning goals to maximize their effectiveness in your daily life.

Chapter 3:

Changing Habits for Lasting Personal Growth

Habits are the building blocks of our daily routines and behaviors, shaping our lives in profound ways. This chapter explores effective strategies and techniques for identifying, modifying, and cultivating new habits to foster lasting personal growth and positive change.

Understanding Habits and Their Impact

Habits are automatic behaviors learned through repetition and reinforcement. They can either support or hinder personal growth, influencing productivity, health, relationships, and overall well-being. Understanding the mechanics of habits is essential for initiating meaningful change.

The Habit Loop: Cue, Routine, Reward

Explore the habit loop—comprising a cue or trigger, a routine or behavior, and a reward—which forms the basis of habit formation. Recognizing these elements helps identify existing habits and facilitates the process of habit modification.

Techniques for Habit Identification

Conduct a habit audit to identify current habits, both beneficial and detrimental, that impact your life. Track behaviors, triggers, and associated rewards to gain insight into patterns and motivations driving your habits.

Setting SMART Goals for Habit Change

Establish Specific, Measurable, Achievable, Relevant, and Time-bound (SMART) goals to guide habit change efforts effectively. Define clear objectives and milestones to track progress and maintain motivation throughout the habit modification process.

Implementing Habit Stacking and Anchoring

Utilize habit stacking by linking new behaviors with existing routines or environmental cues to reinforce desired habits. Anchoring involves associating new habits with specific triggers or situations to facilitate consistency and adherence.

Behavioral Modification Techniques

Apply behavioral modification techniques, such as positive reinforcement, habit substitution, and gradual exposure, to replace undesirable habits with healthier alternatives. Reward progress and celebrate achievements to reinforce new behaviors.

Creating Supportive Environments

Modify your physical and social environments to support desired habit changes. Remove temptations or triggers associated with unwanted habits and surround yourself with individuals who encourage and reinforce positive behaviors.

Overcoming Resistance and Setbacks

Anticipate challenges and setbacks during the habit change process. Develop resilience by learning from setbacks, adjusting strategies as needed, and maintaining commitment to long-term personal growth and development.

Practicing Mindfulness and Self-Reflection

Integrate mindfulness practices and self-reflection into your daily routine to enhance awareness of habits, emotions, and motivations. Mindfulness cultivates intentional decision-making and self-regulation, supporting sustainable habit change.

Embracing Personal Growth Through Habit Change

By adopting effective strategies and techniques for changing habits, you can cultivate lasting personal growth, achieve desired outcomes, and enhance overall well-being. Embrace the journey of habit modification as a pathway to self-improvement, resilience, and fulfillment in various aspects of life.

Changing habits for lasting personal growth involves adopting behaviors that align with your goals and values, fostering continuous improvement and positive transformation. Here are examples of habits you can change to support lasting personal growth:

1. **Daily Reflection**: Allocate time each day for self-reflection and introspection. Reflect on your achievements, challenges, and areas for improvement to cultivate self-awareness and guide personal growth.

2. **Goal Setting**: Establish SMART (Specific, Measurable, Achievable, Relevant, Time-bound) goals that challenge you to stretch beyond your comfort zone. Regularly review and adjust goals to maintain motivation and track progress.

3. **Mindful Eating**: Practice mindful eating by focusing on the sensory experience of eating, recognizing hunger and satiety cues, and making nutritious food choices that support physical and mental well-being.

4. **Regular Exercise Routine**: Incorporate regular physical activity into your routine to promote overall health, reduce stress, and boost energy levels. Choose activities that you enjoy and can sustain over time.

5. **Effective Time Management**: Develop time management skills to prioritize tasks, set deadlines, and allocate time for activities that align with your goals. Use productivity tools and techniques to maximize efficiency and minimize procrastination.

6. **Continuous Learning**: Cultivate a habit of lifelong learning by exploring new subjects, acquiring new skills, or pursuing personal interests. Engage in reading, online courses, workshops, or seminars to expand knowledge and perspectives.

7. **Daily Gratitude Practice**: Dedicate time each day to express gratitude for people, experiences, or blessings in your life. Practicing gratitude promotes positivity, resilience, and a deeper appreciation for everyday moments.

8. **Limiting Screen Time**: Reduce excessive screen time and digital distractions by setting boundaries on device use. Allocate screen-free periods for relaxation, reflection, and meaningful interactions with others.

9. **Journaling**: Keep a journal to record thoughts, emotions, ideas, and insights. Journaling fosters self-expression, clarity of thought, and emotional processing, promoting personal growth and self-discovery.

10. **Seeking Feedback and Self-Improvement**: Embrace feedback as an opportunity for growth and self-improvement. Seek constructive feedback from others, reflect on areas for development, and take proactive steps to enhance skills and behaviors.

By consciously changing these habits and integrating them into your daily life, you can foster lasting personal growth, cultivate resilience, and achieve greater fulfillment in various aspects of your life. Stay committed to continuous improvement and adapt these habits to suit your evolving goals and aspirations.

Chapter 4:

Energizing Your Life: Nutrition, Exercise, and Sleep

Energizing your life requires a holistic approach that encompasses nutrition, exercise, and sleep. This chapter explores how optimizing these fundamental aspects can enhance vitality, promote well-being, and support overall quality of life.

Understanding the Importance of Nutrition

Nutrition plays a crucial role in providing energy and essential nutrients for optimal physical and mental function. Explore the impact of balanced macronutrients, micronutrients, hydration, and mindful eating habits on energy levels and overall health.

Principles of a Balanced Diet

Learn the principles of a balanced diet that includes a variety of fruits, vegetables, whole grains, lean proteins, and healthy fats. Discover the benefits of nutrient-dense foods and moderation in sugar, salt, and processed foods for sustained energy and vitality.

Strategic Meal Planning and Nutrient Timing

Develop strategies for meal planning and nutrient timing to optimize energy levels throughout the day. Consider incorporating small, frequent meals, balanced snacks, and pre- and post-exercise nutrition to support physical performance and recovery.

Exercise: Enhancing Physical Energy and Mental Clarity

Explore the benefits of regular physical activity for enhancing physical energy, mental clarity, and overall well-being. Discover various types of exercise, including aerobic, strength training, flexibility, and balance exercises, to promote vitality and resilience.

Creating an Exercise Routine

Develop a personalized exercise routine that aligns with your fitness goals, preferences, and schedule. Set realistic goals, gradually increase intensity, and incorporate diverse activities to maintain motivation and enjoyment in your fitness journey.

Importance of Sleep for Energy Restoration

Understand the critical role of sleep in energy restoration, cognitive function, and overall health. Explore the stages of sleep, sleep hygiene practices, and strategies for improving sleep quality and duration to support physical and mental well-being.

Sleep Hygiene Practices

Implement sleep hygiene practices, such as establishing a consistent sleep schedule, creating a relaxing bedtime routine, optimizing sleep environment, and limiting exposure to screens and stimulants before bedtime, to promote restorative sleep.

Stress Management and Relaxation Techniques

Incorporate stress management and relaxation techniques, such as mindfulness meditation, deep breathing exercises, progressive muscle relaxation, and hobbies, to reduce stress levels and promote relaxation for improved sleep and overall energy levels.

Hydration and its Impact on Energy

Understand the importance of hydration for maintaining energy levels, cognitive function, and physical performance. Explore strategies for staying adequately hydrated throughout the day and the benefits of water versus sugary beverages.

Embracing a Balanced Lifestyle for Energy and Vitality

By optimizing nutrition, incorporating regular exercise, and prioritizing quality sleep and stress management, you can energize your life and enhance overall well-being. Embrace a balanced lifestyle that supports sustained energy, mental clarity, and resilience to thrive in daily life.

Energizing your life through nutrition, exercise, and sleep involves adopting habits that support physical vitality, mental clarity, and overall well-being. Here are examples of how you can optimize each area:

Nutrition:

1. **Balanced Meals**: Incorporate a variety of nutrient-dense foods such as fruits, vegetables, whole grains, lean proteins, and healthy fats into your diet. Aim for

balanced meals that provide sustained energy throughout the day.

2. **Hydration**: Stay hydrated by drinking plenty of water throughout the day. Opt for water over sugary beverages to maintain hydration levels and support overall bodily functions.

3. **Snack Choices**: Choose healthy snacks like nuts, seeds, yogurt, or fruit to curb hunger and maintain energy levels between meals. Avoid processed snacks high in sugar and unhealthy fats.

4. **Meal Planning**: Plan meals ahead to ensure you have nutritious options readily available. Batch cooking and meal prepping can save time and promote healthier eating habits.

5. **Mindful Eating**: Practice mindful eating by focusing on the sensory experience of food. Chew slowly, savor flavors, and pay attention to hunger and fullness cues to prevent overeating.

Exercise:

1. **Cardiovascular Exercises**: Engage in aerobic activities such as jogging, cycling, swimming, or dancing to

improve cardiovascular health, increase stamina, and boost overall energy levels.

2. **Strength Training**: Incorporate resistance exercises like weightlifting or bodyweight workouts to build muscle strength, enhance metabolism, and improve physical resilience.

3. **Flexibility and Balance**: Include stretching exercises, yoga, or tai chi to improve flexibility, balance, and posture. These activities can reduce stiffness, enhance mobility, and promote relaxation.

4. **Regular Activity**: Aim for at least 150 minutes of moderate-intensity exercise or 75 minutes of vigorous-intensity exercise per week, as recommended by health guidelines, to maintain overall fitness and vitality.

5. **Outdoor Activities**: Take advantage of outdoor activities such as hiking, gardening, or playing sports to increase exposure to natural light, fresh air, and vitamin D, which can uplift mood and enhance energy levels.

Sleep:

1. **Consistent Sleep Schedule**: Establish a regular sleep routine by going to bed and waking up at the same time

each day, even on weekends. Consistency helps regulate your body's internal clock for better sleep quality.

2. **Sleep Environment**: Create a sleep-friendly environment that is dark, quiet, and cool to promote relaxation and minimize disruptions. Use comfortable bedding and consider blackout curtains or white noise machines if needed.

3. **Bedtime Rituals**: Develop calming bedtime rituals such as reading, taking a warm bath, or practicing relaxation techniques like deep breathing or meditation to signal to your body that it's time to wind down.

4. **Limiting Stimulants**: Avoid consuming caffeine, nicotine, and heavy meals close to bedtime, as these can interfere with sleep onset and disrupt sleep cycles.

5. **Quality over Quantity**: Focus on achieving restorative sleep by prioritizing sleep quality over quantity. Aim for 7-9 hours of sleep per night to support cognitive function, mood regulation, and overall well-being.

By incorporating these examples into your lifestyle, you can effectively energize your life, enhance vitality, and promote long-term health and well-being. Adjust these practices to suit your preferences and individual needs, ensuring sustainable habits that contribute to a balanced and fulfilling life.

Chapter 5:

Sharpening Focus: Strategies for Mental Clarity

Achieving mental clarity and enhancing focus are essential for productivity, creativity, and overall well-being. This chapter explores effective strategies and techniques to sharpen your focus, improve concentration, and optimize cognitive performance.

Understanding Mental Clarity and Focus

Explore the concept of mental clarity and its importance in achieving optimal cognitive function. Learn how enhanced focus can boost productivity, decision-making, and problem-solving abilities in various aspects of life.

Mindfulness and Focus

Discover how mindfulness practices, such as meditation, mindful breathing, and body scan exercises, can improve attentional control and mental clarity. Explore the benefits of present-moment awareness in reducing distractions and enhancing focus.

Techniques for Improving Concentration

Learn practical techniques, including time-blocking, Pomodoro Technique, and task prioritization, to improve concentration and minimize multitasking. Develop strategies for managing distractions and maintaining focus on priority tasks.

Environment Optimization

Create a conducive environment for sharpening focus by minimizing clutter, reducing noise distractions, and optimizing lighting and ergonomics. Explore the benefits of workspace organization and establishing a dedicated focus area for productive work.

Cognitive Enhancement Strategies

Engage in cognitive enhancement activities, such as brain games, puzzles, and memory exercises, to stimulate neural pathways and improve cognitive function. Discover the role of continuous learning and intellectual challenges in maintaining mental sharpness.

Nutrition for Cognitive Performance

Understand the impact of nutrition on cognitive performance and focus. Explore dietary strategies that support brain health, including foods rich in antioxidants, omega-3 fatty acids, and vitamins essential for mental clarity and concentration.

Physical Activity and Brain Function

Explore the connection between physical activity and cognitive function. Discover how regular exercise promotes neuroplasticity, enhances mood, and improves focus by increasing blood flow and oxygenation to the brain.

Stress Management and Mental Clarity

Implement stress management techniques, such as deep breathing, progressive muscle relaxation, and mindfulness-based stress reduction, to reduce stress levels and enhance mental clarity. Explore the impact of stress on cognitive function and productivity.

Sleep and Cognitive Function

Prioritize quality sleep to support cognitive function, memory consolidation, and mental clarity. Explore strategies for improving sleep quality and establishing a bedtime routine conducive to restorative sleep and optimal brain function.

Cultivating Mental Clarity for Success

By implementing strategies for sharpening focus and enhancing mental clarity into your daily routine, you can optimize cognitive performance, boost productivity, and achieve greater success in personal and professional endeavors. Embrace the journey of continuous improvement and mindfulness to cultivate a clear and focused mind capable of thriving in today's dynamic world.

Sharpening focus and enhancing mental clarity are crucial for productivity, learning, and overall well-being. Here are effective strategies and examples to help you achieve mental clarity:

1. **Mindfulness Meditation**: Practice mindfulness meditation to improve focus and attention. By training your mind to stay present and observe thoughts without judgment, you can reduce mental distractions and enhance clarity.

2. **Deep Breathing Exercises**: Engage in deep breathing techniques, such as diaphragmatic breathing or box breathing, to calm the mind, increase oxygen flow to the brain, and improve concentration.

3. **Task Prioritization**: Use techniques like Eisenhower's Urgent/Important Principle or the ABCDE Method to prioritize tasks based on their significance and deadlines. This helps reduce overwhelm and allows you to focus on what truly matters.

4. **Time Blocking**: Allocate specific blocks of time for focused work on one task or project at a time. Minimize multitasking to maintain concentration and achieve deeper engagement with the task at hand.

5. **Digital Detox**: Schedule periods throughout the day to disconnect from digital devices and notifications. Limiting screen time reduces mental fatigue and improves concentration by minimizing distractions.

6. **Environment Optimization**: Create a conducive workspace by minimizing clutter, adjusting lighting and temperature, and using ergonomic furniture. A well-organized environment promotes mental clarity and enhances focus.

7. **Regular Physical Activity**: Engage in regular exercise, such as brisk walking, jogging, or yoga, to enhance blood flow to the brain, reduce stress levels, and improve cognitive function, including focus and concentration.

8. **Brain Games and Puzzles**: Challenge your brain with puzzles, crosswords, Sudoku, or logic games to stimulate cognitive function and improve problem-solving skills. These activities promote mental agility and sharpen focus.

9. **Healthy Nutrition**: Maintain a balanced diet rich in brain-boosting nutrients such as omega-3 fatty acids, antioxidants, and vitamins. Proper nutrition supports cognitive function and enhances mental clarity.

10. **Quality Sleep**: Prioritize adequate and restful sleep to consolidate memories, process information, and recharge the brain. Establish a consistent sleep schedule and create a relaxing bedtime routine to optimize sleep quality.

By integrating these strategies into your daily routine, you can sharpen your focus, enhance mental clarity, and optimize cognitive performance. Experiment with different techniques to identify which ones work best for you and adapt them to suit your specific goals and challenges.

Chapter 6:

Transforming Your Brain: Neuroplasticity and Mental Exercises

Understanding neuroplasticity and engaging in targeted mental exercises can profoundly impact brain function and cognitive abilities. This chapter explores how harnessing neuroplasticity through specific exercises and practices can lead to transformative changes in your brain's structure and function.

Exploring Neuroplasticity

Delve into the concept of neuroplasticity, the brain's remarkable ability to reorganize and form new neural connections throughout life in response to learning, experience, and environmental factors. Understand how neuroplasticity underpins learning, memory, and adaptive behaviors.

Principles of Neuroplasticity

Explore the principles of neuroplasticity, including use-dependent plasticity (the idea that neural connections strengthen with repeated use) and neurogenesis (the formation of new neurons), and how these processes support brain health and cognitive flexibility.

Benefits of Mental Exercises

Discover the benefits of engaging in mental exercises and cognitive training to enhance neuroplasticity. Explore how these activities stimulate neural growth, improve information processing speed, and enhance memory retention and recall.

Brain Training Programs

Explore popular brain training programs and apps designed to improve cognitive functions such as attention, memory, problem-solving, and mental agility. Evaluate the effectiveness of structured brain exercises in promoting neuroplasticity and cognitive enhancement.

Memory Enhancement Techniques

Learn specific techniques and mnemonic devices, such as visualization, chunking, and method of loci, to enhance memory retention and recall. Discover how these strategies leverage neuroplasticity to optimize encoding and retrieval processes in the brain.

Cognitive Flexibility and Problem-Solving

Engage in activities that promote cognitive flexibility and problem-solving skills, such as puzzles, logic games, and strategy-based exercises. Explore how challenging mental tasks stimulate adaptive changes in neural networks and enhance cognitive resilience.

Language Learning and Neuroplasticity

Explore the role of language learning in promoting neuroplasticity and cognitive function. Discover how acquiring new languages or practicing multilingualism can strengthen neural connections, improve executive function, and enhance overall brain health.

Meditation and Neuroplasticity

Investigate the impact of mindfulness meditation and other contemplative practices on brain structure and function. Explore research findings on how meditation promotes neuroplasticity, reduces stress-related neural atrophy, and enhances emotional regulation and attentional control.

Lifestyle Factors and Brain Health

Understand how lifestyle factors, including nutrition, physical exercise, sleep quality, and social interaction, influence neuroplasticity and brain health. Explore holistic approaches to supporting cognitive function and optimizing brain performance.

Embracing Brain Transformation

By understanding and harnessing the principles of neuroplasticity through targeted mental exercises and lifestyle practices, you can facilitate transformative changes in your brain's structure and function. Embrace the journey of continuous learning, cognitive enrichment, and neuroplasticity to cultivate a resilient and adaptive brain capable of thriving throughout life's challenges and opportunities.

Transforming your brain through neuroplasticity and mental exercises involves engaging in activities that promote the formation of new neural connections and enhance cognitive function. Here are examples of how you can harness neuroplasticity to transform your brain:

1. **Learning a New Skill**: Challenge your brain by learning a new language, musical instrument, or artistic skill.

Acquiring new knowledge stimulates neuroplasticity and promotes the growth of neural networks associated with learning and memory.

2. **Brain Training Apps**: Use brain training apps and programs designed to improve cognitive functions such as memory, attention, problem-solving, and mental agility. These exercises target specific brain areas and enhance neuroplasticity through repetitive practice.

3. **Mindfulness Meditation**: Practice mindfulness meditation to reshape neural pathways associated with attention, emotional regulation, and stress resilience. Mindfulness promotes neuroplastic changes in the brain's structure and function, supporting mental clarity and well-being.

4. **Physical Exercise**: Engage in regular aerobic exercise, such as running, swimming, or cycling, to boost blood flow to the brain and stimulate neurogenesis (formation of new neurons). Exercise enhances cognitive function, including memory, and supports brain health.

5. **Cognitive Behavioral Therapy (CBT)**: Participate in CBT sessions to reframe negative thought patterns and promote adaptive behaviors. CBT utilizes neuroplasticity

to rewire neural circuits associated with emotional regulation and problem-solving.

6. **Crossword Puzzles and Sudoku**: Challenge your brain with puzzles and games that require critical thinking, memory retrieval, and problem-solving skills. These mental exercises strengthen synaptic connections and improve cognitive flexibility.

7. **Music Therapy**: Engage in music activities such as playing an instrument, singing, or listening to music to stimulate multiple brain regions involved in auditory processing, motor coordination, and emotional expression. Music therapy enhances neuroplasticity and cognitive function.

8. **Reading and Intellectual Engagement**: Read books, articles, or academic journals to expose your brain to new ideas, concepts, and information. Intellectual engagement supports neuroplasticity by promoting synaptic growth and strengthening neural networks associated with learning.

9. **Social Interaction**: Maintain social connections and engage in meaningful conversations and activities with others. Social interaction stimulates brain regions involved in empathy, communication, and emotional

regulation, promoting neuroplastic changes that support cognitive health.

10. **Nutritional Support**: Consume a balanced diet rich in antioxidants, omega-3 fatty acids, and vitamins essential for brain health. Nutrients support neuroplasticity by providing energy for neural processes and protecting neurons from oxidative stress.

By incorporating these examples into your lifestyle, you can harness the power of neuroplasticity to transform your brain, enhance cognitive abilities, and promote lifelong learning and mental resilience. Experiment with different activities to find those that resonate most with you and integrate them into your daily routine for optimal brain health and function.

Chapter 7:

Strengthening Relationships: Communication and Empathy

Effective communication and empathy are foundational to building and maintaining strong, meaningful relationships. This chapter explores strategies and techniques to enhance your communication skills and cultivate empathy, fostering deeper connections with others.

The Importance of Relationships

Understand the significance of relationships in fostering emotional well-being, support, and personal growth. Explore how effective communication and empathy contribute to building trust, resolving conflicts, and creating fulfilling connections.

Components of Effective Communication

Explore the key components of effective communication, including active listening, clarity in expression, nonverbal cues, and assertiveness. Learn how these elements facilitate understanding, promote openness, and strengthen interpersonal bonds.

Active Listening Techniques

Master active listening techniques, such as paraphrasing, reflecting feelings, and asking clarifying questions, to demonstrate empathy and validate others' experiences. Discover how attentive listening enhances communication and promotes mutual respect.

Assertiveness and Setting Boundaries

Develop assertiveness skills to express thoughts, feelings, and needs confidently and respectfully. Explore strategies for setting and maintaining healthy boundaries in relationships to promote mutual understanding and respect.

Nonverbal Communication and Body Language

Understand the role of nonverbal communication and body language in conveying emotions, intentions, and attitudes. Learn to interpret and use nonverbal cues effectively to enhance communication and strengthen interpersonal connections.

Conflict Resolution Strategies

Explore constructive approaches to resolving conflicts and disagreements in relationships. Learn techniques for active problem-solving, compromise, and negotiation to achieve mutually beneficial outcomes and preserve relationship harmony.

Cultivating Empathy

Develop empathy as a cornerstone of emotional intelligence and relationship building. Explore the ability to understand and share others' emotions, perspectives, and experiences, fostering compassion, connection, and mutual support.

Perspective-Taking and Empathetic Listening

Practice perspective-taking to understand situations from others' viewpoints and cultivate empathetic listening skills. Learn how empathy promotes deeper understanding, strengthens emotional bonds, and nurtures trust in relationships.

Emotional Regulation and Empathy

Explore the connection between emotional regulation and empathy. Learn techniques for managing your own emotions effectively to remain empathetic and supportive in challenging or emotionally charged interactions.

Nurturing Meaningful Connections

By honing communication skills, practicing empathy, and fostering emotional intelligence, you can cultivate and strengthen meaningful relationships. Embrace the journey of understanding, connection, and mutual growth to build lasting bonds and enrich your life with meaningful connections.

Strengthening relationships through effective communication and empathy is essential for building trust, fostering connection, and resolving conflicts constructively. Here are examples of how to enhance relationships through communication and empathy:

1. **Active Listening**: Practice active listening by giving your full attention to the speaker, maintaining eye contact, and reflecting back what you've heard to ensure understanding. For example, paraphrasing their main points to show you're listening.
2. **Empathetic Responses**: Respond empathetically by acknowledging the other person's feelings and

perspectives. For instance, saying, "I can see why you feel that way," demonstrates empathy and validates their emotions.

3. **Open and Honest Communication**: Foster open communication by expressing your thoughts, feelings, and concerns honestly and respectfully. For example, using "I" statements like "I feel..." instead of "You always..." promotes understanding and reduces defensiveness.

4. **Conflict Resolution Skills**: Develop conflict resolution skills by actively seeking solutions that meet the needs of both parties. For example, using "win-win" negotiation techniques and compromising on smaller issues can lead to mutually beneficial outcomes.

5. **Nonverbal Communication**: Pay attention to nonverbal cues such as facial expressions, gestures, and body language, as they often convey emotions and intentions more accurately than words alone. For example, noticing when someone looks uncomfortable and checking in with them.

6. **Respectful Disagreement**: Respectfully disagree by acknowledging differing opinions without undermining or dismissing the other person's perspective. For instance,

saying, "I see your point, but I have a different perspective" encourages open dialogue and mutual respect.

7. **Sharing Appreciation**: Express appreciation and gratitude for the other person's contributions, qualities, or efforts in the relationship. For example, thanking them for their support during a challenging time or acknowledging their strengths.

8. **Setting Boundaries**: Establish healthy boundaries by clearly communicating your needs, limits, and expectations in the relationship. For instance, politely declining invitations when you need time for self-care demonstrates self-respect and maintains balance.

9. **Quality Time Together**: Dedicate quality time to connect and strengthen bonds through shared activities or meaningful conversations. For example, scheduling regular date nights or family dinners to nurture relationships and create lasting memories.

10. **Apologizing and Forgiving**: Practice genuine apologies by taking responsibility for mistakes and showing remorse. Similarly, offer forgiveness when appropriate to let go of resentment and rebuild trust in the relationship.

By incorporating these examples into your interactions, you can cultivate strong, healthy relationships based on effective communication, empathy, and mutual respect. Building these skills over time fosters deeper connections, enhances understanding, and promotes a supportive and fulfilling relationship dynamic.

Chapter 8:

Integrating Mindfulness and Stress Management

Mindfulness and effective stress management are essential tools for maintaining mental well-being and resilience in today's fast-paced world. This chapter explores how integrating mindfulness practices can enhance stress management techniques, promoting overall health and emotional balance.

Understanding Mindfulness

Delve into the concept of mindfulness as the practice of being present in the moment with non-judgmental awareness. Explore how mindfulness cultivates heightened awareness of thoughts, emotions, and bodily sensations, fostering clarity and emotional resilience.

Benefits of Mindfulness for Stress Reduction

Explore the benefits of mindfulness in reducing stress levels and promoting relaxation. Learn how mindfulness practices, such as meditation, mindful breathing, and body scan exercises, enhance self-regulation and improve coping mechanisms in stressful situations.

Techniques for Practicing Mindfulness

Discover practical techniques for integrating mindfulness into daily life. Explore formal practices, such as sitting meditation and guided mindfulness sessions, as well as informal practices, like mindful eating, walking, and everyday mindfulness in activities.

Mindfulness-Based Stress Reduction (MBSR)

Learn about Mindfulness-Based Stress Reduction (MBSR) programs designed to cultivate mindfulness skills and resilience in managing stress. Explore the structured approach of MBSR, including meditation practices, yoga, and cognitive-behavioral techniques.

Applying Mindfulness to Workplace Stress

Explore how mindfulness can be applied to manage workplace stress effectively. Learn techniques for staying present and focused amidst pressure, fostering collaborative relationships, and promoting a supportive work environment.

Stress Management Techniques

Explore complementary stress management techniques, such as progressive muscle relaxation, deep breathing exercises, and visualization, to reduce physiological arousal and promote relaxation responses.

Cognitive Restructuring and Stress

Understand cognitive restructuring techniques to challenge and reframe stress-inducing thoughts and beliefs. Explore how changing perspectives and cultivating resilience through mindfulness can transform stress into opportunities for growth.

Self-Compassion and Stress Resilience

Develop self-compassion as a cornerstone of effective stress management. Explore practices for treating yourself with kindness and understanding during challenging times, fostering emotional resilience and inner strength.

Integrating Mindfulness into Daily Routine

Develop a personalized mindfulness routine that integrates formal and informal practices into your daily life. Explore strategies for consistency and sustainability in mindfulness practice to reap long-term benefits for stress management and overall well-being.

Embracing Mindfulness for Stress Management

By integrating mindfulness practices into your life and mastering effective stress management techniques, you can enhance resilience, promote emotional balance, and cultivate a greater sense of well-being. Embrace the transformative power of mindfulness to navigate life's challenges with clarity, presence, and compassion.

Integrating mindfulness into stress management practices can significantly enhance your ability to cope with challenges and maintain overall well-being. Here are examples of how to integrate mindfulness into your daily life for effective stress management:

1. **Mindful Breathing**: Take breaks throughout the day to focus on your breath. Practice deep breathing exercises, such as diaphragmatic breathing or box breathing, to calm the mind and reduce stress levels.
2. **Body Scan Meditation**: Engage in body scan meditation to systematically relax each part of your body and release

tension. Start from your toes and work your way up to your head, noticing any sensations without judgment.

3. **Mindful Walking**: Practice mindful walking by paying attention to each step, the movement of your body, and the sensations of walking. Use this practice during breaks or outdoor activities to cultivate present-moment awareness.

4. **Mindful Eating**: Slow down and savor each bite during meals. Notice the flavors, textures, and sensations of eating without distractions. This practice enhances digestion, promotes mindful food choices, and reduces stress related to eating.

5. **Mindful Communication**: Practice mindful communication by listening actively and responding with awareness. Pause before speaking to consider your words and intentions, fostering clearer and more compassionate interactions.

6. **Mindful Work Breaks**: Take short mindfulness breaks during work to reset and recharge. Use apps or reminders to prompt brief periods of mindfulness practice, such as focusing on your breath or surroundings for a few minutes.

7. **Mindful Stress Response**: When faced with stressors, pause and observe your thoughts and emotions without reacting impulsively. Practice responding mindfully by choosing thoughtful actions or taking a moment to breathe before proceeding.

8. **Mindful Movement**: Engage in mindful movement practices such as yoga, tai chi, or stretching exercises. Focus on the sensations of movement, breath, and body alignment to promote relaxation and reduce physical tension.

9. **Mindful Technology Use**: Set boundaries on digital device use to reduce distractions and promote mindfulness. Practice mindful tech habits by taking breaks, setting intentions for screen time, and limiting exposure to stressful content.

10. **Mindfulness in Daily Activities**: Infuse mindfulness into routine activities such as washing dishes, commuting, or doing household chores. Use these moments to anchor yourself in the present and cultivate a sense of calm and clarity.

By integrating these mindfulness practices into your daily routine, you can effectively manage stress, improve resilience, and enhance overall well-being. Start with small steps and gradually incorporate these techniques to experience the benefits of mindfulness in reducing stress and promoting a more balanced life.

Chapter 9:

Sustaining Your Mind Rewiring Journey

Embarking on a journey to rewire your mind involves ongoing commitment and dedication to personal growth and well-being. This chapter explores strategies and principles for sustaining your mind rewiring journey over the long term, ensuring lasting positive changes in various aspects of your life.

Embracing Lifelong Learning and Growth

Understand the importance of embracing lifelong learning and growth as integral to sustaining your mind rewiring journey. Explore the mindset of continuous improvement, curiosity, and openness to new experiences as catalysts for personal transformation.

Reflecting on Progress and Achievements

Develop a habit of reflecting on your progress and celebrating achievements along your mind rewiring journey. Explore techniques for acknowledging milestones, identifying areas for growth, and maintaining motivation through positive reinforcement.

Establishing Supportive Habits and Routines

Create supportive habits and routines that reinforce your mind rewiring goals. Explore strategies for integrating mindfulness practices, healthy lifestyle habits, and productive routines into your daily life to sustain positive changes and enhance well-being.

Setting Meaningful Goals and Intentions

Set meaningful goals and intentions aligned with your values and aspirations. Learn how to establish SMART goals (Specific, Measurable, Achievable, Relevant, and Time-bound) to maintain focus, track progress, and cultivate a sense of purpose throughout your journey.

Practicing Self-Compassion and Resilience

Cultivate self-compassion and resilience as essential qualities for navigating challenges and setbacks along your mind rewiring journey. Explore practices for self-care, managing stress, and responding to difficulties with kindness and perseverance.

Building and Nurturing Supportive Relationships

Foster supportive relationships that encourage and inspire your personal growth. Explore the importance of connection, communication, and empathy in sustaining motivation, sharing experiences, and receiving encouragement from others.

Continuing Education and Skill Development

Engage in continuing education and skill development to expand knowledge and abilities relevant to your mind rewiring goals. Explore opportunities for learning, acquiring new skills, and applying insights to enhance personal and professional growth.

Managing Challenges and Adversities

Develop strategies for managing challenges and adversities that may arise during your mind rewiring journey. Explore resilience-building techniques, problem-solving skills, and adaptive coping strategies to overcome obstacles and maintain momentum.

Integrating Mindfulness into Daily Life

Integrate mindfulness into your daily life as a foundational practice for sustaining mental clarity, emotional balance, and resilience. Explore techniques for staying present, managing stress, and fostering well-being amidst daily responsibilities and pressures.

Embracing the Journey of Mind Rewiring

By embracing strategies for sustaining your mind rewiring journey, you can cultivate lasting positive changes, enhance well-being, and achieve personal fulfillment. Embrace the ongoing process of growth, self-discovery, and transformation to lead a purposeful and meaningful life aligned with your values and aspirations.

Sustaining your mind rewiring journey involves integrating habits and practices that support long-term growth, resilience, and well-being. Here are examples of how to sustain your journey of personal development and transformation:

1. **Daily Mindfulness Practice**: Dedicate time each day to practice mindfulness meditation or other mindfulness

techniques to maintain mental clarity, reduce stress, and enhance self-awareness.

2. **Journaling**: Keep a journal to reflect on your progress, insights, and challenges encountered during your mind rewiring journey. Write down gratitude lists, affirmations, or reflections on personal growth to stay motivated and focused.

3. **Regular Physical Activity**: Incorporate regular exercise into your routine to boost mood, improve cognitive function, and promote overall well-being. Choose activities you enjoy, such as walking, yoga, or dancing, to make exercise a sustainable habit.

4. **Healthy Nutrition**: Maintain a balanced diet rich in nutrients that support brain health and energy levels. Fuel your body with whole foods, fruits, vegetables, lean proteins, and healthy fats to sustain your energy throughout the day.

5. **Continued Learning and Skill Development**: Engage in lifelong learning by exploring new interests, taking courses, or acquiring skills that align with your personal and professional goals. Continual growth stimulates the brain and fosters a sense of accomplishment.

6. **Supportive Relationships**: Nurture relationships with supportive friends, family members, or mentors who encourage your personal growth journey. Seek guidance, share experiences, and celebrate milestones together.

7. **Self-Care Rituals**: Establish regular self-care practices such as relaxation techniques, hot baths, or hobbies that promote stress relief and rejuvenation. Prioritize self-care to maintain emotional balance and resilience.

8. **Setting and Reviewing Goals**: Set specific, measurable goals aligned with your values and aspirations. Regularly review your goals, track progress, and adjust strategies as needed to stay motivated and focused on your journey.

9. **Community and Accountability**: Join communities, support groups, or accountability partnerships where you can share challenges, receive feedback, and stay accountable to your goals. Collaborative efforts can provide motivation and encouragement.

10. **Adaptability and Resilience**: Cultivate adaptability and resilience to navigate setbacks or challenges that may arise during your mind rewiring journey. Embrace setbacks as learning opportunities and maintain a positive outlook on your growth process.

By integrating these sustainable practices into your lifestyle, you can continue to foster personal growth, enhance well-being, and sustain the positive changes initiated through your mind rewiring journey. Consistency, self-awareness, and a commitment to lifelong learning will empower you to navigate challenges and thrive in your pursuit of a fulfilling life.

Conclusion:

Embracing a Transformed Life

As we conclude this journey of mind rewiring, it becomes clear that transformation is not just about changing habits or adopting new practices—it's about embracing a fundamentally different way of experiencing life. Throughout this book, we've explored strategies for enhancing mood, boosting memory, changing habits, energizing life, sharpening focus, transforming the brain, strengthening relationships, integrating mindfulness, and sustaining personal growth. Each chapter has been a stepping stone toward a more vibrant and fulfilled existence.

Embracing a transformed life means embodying the principles of continuous learning, resilience, and self-awareness. It involves nurturing meaningful relationships, managing stress effectively, and prioritizing self-care. By rewiring our minds, we've empowered ourselves to navigate challenges with clarity, respond to setbacks with resilience, and pursue our aspirations with purpose.

Remember, transformation is a journey, not a destination. It requires patience, commitment, and a willingness to embrace discomfort as a catalyst for growth. As you continue on your path, cultivate gratitude for how far you've come and curiosity for what lies ahead. Embrace the lessons learned, celebrate your achievements, and stay open to new possibilities.

Ultimately, embracing a transformed life means living authentically, aligned with your values and aspirations. It means cultivating inner peace, joy, and a sense of purpose that radiates outward into every aspect of your life. May this journey of mind rewiring continue to inspire and empower you, as you navigate life's complexities with renewed clarity and optimism.

Here's to embracing a transformed life—one filled with resilience, compassion, and the endless potential of a rewired mind.

Bonus:

Positive Daily Affirmations

Here are some positive daily affirmations that relate to the themes of the book title "Rewire Your Mind: Enhance Mood, Boost Memory, Change Your Habits. Energize Your Life and Sharpen Focus. Transform Your Brain while Strengthening Relationships":

1. **Enhance Mood and Boost Memory**:
   - "I am capable of enhancing my mood and boosting my memory through positive daily habits."
   - "Each day, I strengthen my mind and uplift my spirits with positive thoughts."
   - "My mind is resilient and capable of learning and remembering with ease."

2. **Change Your Habits**:
   - "I embrace change and cultivate habits that nurture my mind and body."
   - "I am committed to replacing old habits with new, positive ones that support my well-being."
   - "Every day, I take small steps towards positive change and personal growth."

3. **Energize Your Life and Sharpen Focus**:
   - "I fuel my body with nutritious food and energize my life with healthy habits."
   - "I focus my mind on important tasks and achieve clarity and productivity."
   - "I am full of energy and vitality, ready to tackle any challenges that come my way."

4. **Transform Your Brain**:
   - "I embrace neuroplasticity and actively transform my brain for greater mental agility."
   - "Every day, I engage in activities that stimulate my brain and enhance cognitive function."
   - "My brain is capable of remarkable growth and adaptation."

5. **Strengthening Relationships**:
   - "I communicate openly and empathetically, strengthening my relationships every day."
   - "I nurture meaningful connections with understanding and compassion."
   - "My relationships grow stronger as I prioritize communication and empathy."

6. **Overall Mind Rewiring**:

- "I am rewiring my mind for positivity, resilience, and personal growth."
- "I embrace the journey of self-improvement and celebrate my progress."
- "Every day, I am transforming my life through focused intention and mindful actions."

These affirmations can be personalized and repeated daily to reinforce positive beliefs and support the themes of personal development and well-being addressed in the book "Rewire Your Mind."

Sample Journalizing Strategy:

Rewiring Your Mind for Personal Growth

Date: [Date]

1. Enhance Mood, Boost Memory:

- Today, I noticed improvements in my mood when I practiced [specific positive thinking technique]. Reflect on how this impacted your day.
- What memory-boosting activities did I engage in today? How did they make me feel?

2. Change Your Habits:

- Describe one habit you successfully changed or worked on today. What steps did you take to implement this change?
- Reflect on any challenges faced while trying to change habits. How did I overcome them?

3. Energize Your Life, Sharpen Focus:

- How did I prioritize nutrition, exercise, or sleep today to energize my body and mind?
- Describe a moment when I felt particularly focused and productive. What strategies helped me achieve this state?

4. Transform Your Brain:

- Engage in a brain-training exercise today (e.g., crossword puzzles, mindfulness practice). Reflect on how it challenged your brain and contributed to your mental clarity.

- How have I noticed changes in my thinking patterns or problem-solving abilities since beginning this journey?

5. Strengthening Relationships:

- Describe a positive interaction I had today that strengthened a relationship. What communication or empathy skills did I apply?
- Reflect on a challenge in a relationship. How did I approach it differently using what I've learned?

Additional Prompts:

- What are my current goals for personal growth and mind rewiring? How can I break them down into actionable steps?
- How do I feel overall about my progress on this journey? What adjustments or improvements would I like to make moving forward?

Conclusion:

- Summarize the day's reflections and insights. What have I learned about myself and my ability to rewire my mind?
- Write down a positive affirmation or intention to carry forward into tomorrow.

Tips for Effective Journaling:

- **Consistency:** Aim to journal daily or regularly to track progress and reinforce positive habits.
- **Honesty:** Be honest with yourself about your thoughts, feelings, and challenges.

- **Reflection:** Take time to reflect on both successes and areas for improvement.
- **Gratitude:** Include moments of gratitude to foster a positive mindset and appreciation for progress.

This journaling strategy is designed to align with the themes of personal growth, cognitive enhancement, and relationship building addressed in "Rewire Your Mind." Adjust the prompts and structure as needed to fit your personal journey and experiences.

Strength Prayer for Mind Rewiring:

As I embark on the journey to rewire my mind, I ask for your guidance, strength, and clarity.

Grant me the courage to enhance my mood and boost my memory through positive thoughts and actions. Help me cultivate a mindset of optimism and resilience, even in the face of challenges.

Give me the determination to change my habits for lasting personal growth. May I embrace new behaviors that nurture my well-being and align with my values.

Provide me with the energy and vitality to energize my life and sharpen my focus. Help me prioritize self-care, healthy nutrition, exercise, and restful sleep to support my mental clarity and physical well-being.

Guide me in transforming my brain through neuroplasticity and mental exercises. May I engage in activities that challenge and strengthen my cognitive abilities, fostering lifelong learning and adaptation.

Bless my efforts in strengthening relationships through effective communication and empathy. Grant me the wisdom to nurture meaningful connections and resolve conflicts with compassion and understanding.

Throughout this journey, may I remain open to growth, resilient in adversity, and grateful for each step forward. Help me embrace a transformed life, where I am empowered to live fully and authentically.

Thank you for your guidance and support on this path of personal evolution. May I continue to shine light on my inner strength and embrace the positive changes ahead. Amen.

References

1. **Introduction: Understanding the Power of Mind Rewiring**

   o This section may draw upon introductory texts on neuroscience, psychology, and personal development.

   o References:

     - Doidge, N. (2007). *The Brain That Changes Itself: Stories of Personal Triumph from the Frontiers of Brain Science*. Penguin Books.

     - Siegel, D. J. (2010). *The Mindful Brain: Reflection and Attunement in the Cultivation of Well-Being*. W. W. Norton & Company.

2. **Chapter 1: Enhancing Mood Through Positive Thinking**

   o Focuses on positive psychology, cognitive-behavioral techniques, and the impact of mindset on mood.

   o References:

- Seligman, M. E. P. (2006). *Learned Optimism: How to Change Your Mind and Your Life*. Vintage.
- Fredrickson, B. L. (2009). *Positivity: Top-Notch Research Reveals the Upward Spiral That Will Change Your Life*. Crown.

3. **Chapter 2: Techniques to Boost Memory and Cognitive Function**
   - Explores memory enhancement strategies, cognitive training methods, and brain health.
   - References:
     - Medina, J. (2008). *Brain Rules: 12 Principles for Surviving and Thriving at Work, Home, and School*. Pear Press.
     - Squire, L. R., & Kandel, E. R. (2009). *Memory: From Mind to Molecules*. Roberts & Company Publishers.

4. **Chapter 3: Changing Habits for Lasting Personal Growth**
   - Addresses habit formation, behavior change theories, and practical steps for personal development.
   - References:

- Duhigg, C. (2012). *The Power of Habit: Why We Do What We Do in Life and Business*. Random House.
- Clear, J. (2018). *Atomic Habits: An Easy & Proven Way to Build Good Habits & Break Bad Ones*. Avery.

5. **Chapter 4: Energizing Your Life: Nutrition, Exercise, and Sleep**
   - Covers nutrition science, exercise physiology, and the importance of sleep for cognitive function.
   - References:
     - Gu, F., & Chau, L. (2018). *Nutrition and Enhanced Sports Performance: Muscle Building, Endurance, and Strength*. Academic Press.
     - Walker, M. (2017). *Why We Sleep: Unlocking the Power of Sleep and Dreams*. Scribner.

6. **Chapter 5: Sharpening Focus: Strategies for Mental Clarity**
   - Discusses attentional control, mindfulness practices, and cognitive enhancement techniques.
   - References:

- Goleman, D., & Davidson, R. J. (2017). *Altered Traits: Science Reveals How Meditation Changes Your Mind, Brain, and Body*. Avery.
- Csikszentmihalyi, M. (2008). *Flow: The Psychology of Optimal Experience*. Harper Perennial Modern Classics.

7. **Chapter 6: Transforming Your Brain: Neuroplasticity and Mental Exercises**

   o Explores neuroplasticity research, brain training exercises, and cognitive rehabilitation techniques.

   o References:

      - Begley, S. (2007). *Train Your Mind, Change Your Brain: How a New Science Reveals Our Extraordinary Potential to Transform Ourselves*. Ballantine Books.
      - Merzenich, M. (2013). *Soft-Wired: How the New Science of Brain Plasticity Can Change Your Life*. Parnassus Publishing.

8. **Chapter 7: Strengthening Relationships: Communication and Empathy**

- Focuses on interpersonal communication skills, empathy development, and relationship psychology.
- References:
  - Gottman, J. M., & Silver, N. (2015). *The Seven Principles for Making Marriage Work: A Practical Guide from the Country's Foremost Relationship Expert*. Harmony.
  - Covey, S. R. (2004). *The 7 Habits of Highly Effective People: Powerful Lessons in Personal Change*. Free Press.

9. **Chapter 8: Integrating Mindfulness and Stress Management**
   - Covers mindfulness-based stress reduction (MBSR), relaxation techniques, and stress physiology.
   - References:
     - Kabat-Zinn, J. (2013). *Full Catastrophe Living: Using the Wisdom of Your Body and Mind to Face Stress, Pain, and Illness*. Bantam.
     - Hayes, S. C., Strosahl, K. D., & Wilson, K. G. (2011). *Acceptance and Commitment*

Therapy, Second Edition: The Process and Practice of Mindful Change. The Guilford Press.

10. **Chapter 9: Sustaining Your Mind Rewiring Journey**
    - Explores habits for maintaining personal growth, resilience-building strategies, and lifelong learning principles.
    - References:
        - Duckworth, A. L. (2016). *Grit: The Power of Passion and Perseverance*. Scribner.
        - Dweck, C. S. (2007). *Mindset: The New Psychology of Success*. Ballantine Books.

11. **Conclusion: Embracing a Transformed Life**
    - Summarizes key insights and encourages application of learned principles for personal transformation.
    - References:
        - Covey, S. R. (2004). *The 8th Habit: From Effectiveness to Greatness*. Free Press.
        - Brown, B. (2015). *Rising Strong: How the Ability to Reset Transforms the Way We Live, Love, Parent, and Lead*. Random House.

About the Authors:

Brooke Richardson and Lartina Jones are life experienced.

These references provide a foundation for understanding and implementing the concepts discussed in each chapter, supporting the book's overarching theme of personal growth, cognitive enhancement, and well-being through mind rewiring techniques.

Acknowledgments:

Special thanks to our supporters who helped shape our lives and this transformative guide.

Made in the USA
Columbia, SC
30 July 2024

39604133R00046